Ngalak

We

Yongka

Kangaroo

Miyak

Moon

Koorliny

Going

An old story retold by
Kim Scott, Graeme Miniter and
Wirlomin Noongar Language and Stories

With artwork by
Glenda Williams and Boydan Coyne

Kim Scott.
Photo by Nic Duncan.

Graeme Miniter.
Photo by Gaylene Galardi.

Glenda Williams.
hoto by Gaylene Galardi.

Boydan Coyne.
Photo by Gaylene Galardi.

Ngalak Yongka Miyak Koorliny

The Wirlomin Noongar Language and Stories Project is a not-for-profit cultural organisation and relies on the efforts and talent of its reference group and committee. At the time of writing this includes elders Elaine Miniter, Olivia Roberts, Darryl Williams, Iris Woods, Maureen Farmer, Henry Dabb, Connie Moses, Graeme Miniter, Helen 'Ing' Hall, Roma Winmar, Ezzard Flowers, and Kim Scott, and committee members Gaye Roberts, Glenda Williams, Ted Farmer, Cass Lynch, Mary Gimondo and Lefki Kailis. The input, support and involvement from the wider network of Wirlomin members has also been crucial, and we are proud of long-time members who are gaining the confidence to get involved in events and presentations on a regular basis.

We would also like to thank the Australian Research Council and Curtin University, who partner with Wirlomin to make books like these, and our long-term publishing partners UWAP. We'd like to thank Mary Gimondo and Lefki Kailis for nearly two decades of volunteer efforts, and thank Curtin Research Officer Gaylene Galardi of Curtin University for generously giving her time over the past three years.

For further information, or to listen to an audio reading of this story, go to www.wirlomin.com.au.

You was there.

Demangka-maanga, nganang moort.
Ancestors my family

Remember?

Yoowarl koorl, yoowarl koorl.
Come this way come this way

There was *Demi* Lomas, Djinong and Ing, Dongup and Tjinjel and Tommy Scott. And Binian and Udel and Boomer and Tarr-tarr too.

Boydan and Gaye, Harry Brown and Hazel … of course, *Kayang* Hazel was there.

You musta been there.

We was on a bus.

Ngalak kaalak koorliny.
We home going/moving

Remember? Yeah, we all got off the bus at Jerramungup for a feed. *Kayang* Hazel said that coming home was, well ...

Koora kaalak koora koorliny.
Before/long ago home returning

She said, first time she drove Hopetoun to Ravensthorpe it was night-time and these little min-min lights appeared other side of the fence-line, just across the road. Like a bunch of diamonds in the darkness, racing along with the car.

Kayang was a little girl, resting her head and her hand against the glass, watching the lights flying along with her, just out of reach.

Min-min. *Ben ben bardlanginy.*
Moving lights Little lights travelling

Back on the bus we went down the slope to the Gairdner River. Misty rain – *toorl* – all around, but just before we crossed the river, we turned into Monkey Rock Road and the clouds went away and the sun shone on pools of water strung between the sand and rock of the riverbed.

Toorl	*wort koorl.*	*Bilya*	*Boodja,*	*boya,*	*kep bilawin.*
Mist	away go.	River	Country,	rock,	water glittering/shining

We drove along past that plaque to some of the Old People – you seen that, unna, that plaque – where *Kayang* wrote:

Ngalang	*demangka*	*wirn*	*nidja*	*Boodja*	*nyininy.*
Our	ancestors	spirit	this	Country	sitting/being

Ngalang Demangka
mangka
wirn nitja Boodjar
Nyininy

There are a lot of graves beside the river. The Old People and the ashes of their fires are in the earth beneath our feet. We blossom and bloom, fade and fall.

Ngalak yoort-ak yira koorliny. Baalang maya koora koorliny.
We ashes-of up moving Their sound returning

We camped at the pools and the big rock. *Yongka, yoorn, kaarda* there.
'Roo bobtail goanna

Nyingarn too. We set up camp and had a feed.
Echidna

Just after dark, *Demi* Lomas said, '*ngalak yongka miyak koorliny*'.
we 'roo moon going

Kedalak yey.
Night now

Night-time.

The bus rolled from the campsite and through the windows, we saw the moon rising. It bounced behind bushes and in between trees, jumped at us at every crossroad and driveway, and only started to behave itself as the bus pulled up to a gate.

Miyak wabiny.
Moon playing

Beyond was a large paddock and a sloping hill.

One of the boys opened the gate and we followed *Demi* Lomas.

The moon hung large and shimmering in the sky. Silver straw crunched under our feet, and we walked between hulking shadows in the moonlight.

Miyak	*koombar*	*worl-ak*	*wariny*	*worl-ak*	*nyininy.*
Moon	big	sky-of	hanging	sky-of	sitting/being

We walked to the top of the hill and stood on the wide dome of rock, our shadows sharp in the moonlight, the moon big in the sky.

Demi pointed to the shining circles and half-circles, the crescents and slivers scattered where the water was held in shining, shapely puddles.

Shapes that showed the moon waxing and waning.

How it grows and dies and grows again. All there in the rock.

Baalap boya-k nyininy.
They rock-in sitting/being

Demi showed us a long shape in the rock just like a *yongka* leaves in the sand when it rests there a long time.

Nidja yongka.
This/here 'roo

Nidja miyak.
This/here moon

'*Yongka* lying here. Musta been tired – some people say he been all day jumpin' up at the moon. Anyways, he was tired and he was sad.'

Yongka said to the moon:

'I'm gunna die. I'm gunna die and my bones lie dry and silver in your light. Rain and sun will crack and break these bones, and the grass and the hill grow up around me.'

'True,' said the Moon. 'True.'

'You?' asked *Yongka*. 'Do you die?'

Nidja Yongka Miyak Boodja.

This/here 'roo moon Country

'No,' said the Moon.

'I never die. I never die. I get sick, and I get skinny – skinny like a bone or fingernail in the sky – and I go away, but I come back again as big as ever. I always come back; I grow and shrink, I shine and fade away. But I never die.'

Ngalak nidja boodja nyininy, yey koora boordawan.
We this Country sitting/being now long-ago in the future

Moonlight showered over us, over *Demi*, and shone in the puddles scattered around us and all out of sequence.

Little Mi-Mi asked, 'What about us? We gunna die?'

'Miyak-el-ang-iny', said *Demi*.

‘We say *miyakelanginy* for the moon-shining.’

Miyakelanginy min-min.

Kayang told us about min-min lights racing along with her.

Some people say those lights come from here.

Demi took little Mi-Mi's hand.

'See? Here? That moon rising in your fingernail.

Miyak biri-k nyininy.
Moon fingernail-in sitting/being

You carry a part of this story with you, always.'

We got back on the bus. You close up the book.

Ali kenyak yey.
All finish now

Family members, Elders, and guests at a Wirlomin illustration workshop at Gilcreek Scout Camp in Albany in April 2023.

Ngalak Yongka Miyak Koorliny

BY KIM SCOTT

The Yongka Miyak story is very old, and of a particular place. A Wirlomin ancestor showed its grassy valley to Mr Hassell in the year 1849 before things went awry, and it was not until around 2000 that our elders – Hazel Brown, Lomas Roberts and Audrey Brown – took a group of us back there.

The site is on privately-owned land, and we went up to the new homestead to advise them we were visiting. They know some of our Wirlomin family and a bit of the history and we had a good talk with them in the yard. Then our elders led us past the woodheap to a collapsing, corrugated iron shed.

'We had a special relationship with the Hassell family,' one of them said, and showed us a room with a small fireplace, and another room in which all twelve of them slept. They pointed in the distance to where the dance grounds were, and then they took us to where Yongka Miyak is imprinted in granite.

We are not the first to publish a version of this old story. Ethel Hassell (Mr Hassell's daughter-in-law) wrote about what she called 'Younger and Maak' in her book, *My Dusky Friends* (C.W. Hassell, 1975). Our countrywoman Carol Petterson has also published a version, *Yongka Miyak* (Batchelor Press, 2007). Self-taught anthropologist Daisy Bates recorded a version called 'Meeka and Yong-gur', which was published in the Albany Advertiser in 1930. Lomas Roberts Sr. gave a handwritten version to Roma Winmar, who used it with students at Moorditj College. Video footage of Lomas Roberts and Graeme Miniter with small groups of Wirlomin at Yongka Miyak can be found on our website.

The circle of people around any story widens and its centre can move too, but the heart of this story – its resistant nub, if you like – remains a particular place.

Ethel Hassell knew the location of the site. 'About a mile from the homestead', she writes, and in the same pages boasts of the thick stone walls of a homestead 'built as a fort' and 'quite capable of withstanding a siege'. She also mentions a secure room where the guns and powder were kept. Such detail suggests an historical context and truth, and why the location of the story was almost lost to us.

'It is a very special place …' Freddy Yinmer told Aunty Audrey when he took her there, '… for very special people'. Aunty Audrey was only a girl then, and of course, they are all long gone now.

The old stone homestead remains, close to the creek. Vast rectangles of low crops or bare earth stretch from its attendant buildings all the way to the horizon, interrupted only by the thin bitumen road, and an occasional granite dome capping some slope. Yongka Miyak is on one such granite dome. There, imprinted in the granite, is the shape of a kangaroo. Not the silhouette exactly, more the mark a kangaroo leaves when it rests again and again at the same place; something like a roughly drawn capital 'C', wider at the ends, narrow in the middle, the trace of a tail. Weed and dry grass sometimes make the kangaroo hard to see; let alone the circles, the half-circles, slivers and crescents imprinted in the granite rock around it.

Perhaps drone footage would help conceptualise the story as it wants to be told, but let me tell you of the night I visited the site shortly after rain. I stood on the hilltop with Lomas Roberts under a full moon, and light reflected from small, shapely pools all around us. *'Miyak-el-ang-iny,'* said Uncle Lomas. To an amateur linguist such as myself, it's an unusual Noongar construction – noun, rather than verb, followed by such suffixes. 'The moon shining,' Uncle Lomas translated. Surrounded by broken, glittering moons it seemed that time itself might go awry, and the brimming light hum some sort of Country-speak. But we were on the road and weary and we kept moving.

LANGUAGE AND LAYOUT

The Noongar language in this book mostly follows the spelling recommended by both The West Australian Education Department and the Noongar Boodjar Language Cultural Aboriginal Corporation. Material donated by Hazel Brown, Lomas Roberts, Audrey Brown and – to a lesser extent – Albert Knapp, is at the heart of our vocabulary and pronunciation. The handwritten wordlist Hazel Brown compiled with her father, Fred Tjinjel Roberts, in the late 20th century remains an inspiration for Wirlomin Noongar Language and Stories. Workshopping our little archive with extended family has increased the value of the original contributions. Public archival material, primarily from the Gerhardt Laves Noongar Language notes and Daisy Bates' Noongar wordlists from along the south coast of WA, supplements the above. Of published Noongar language publications and wordlists, Wirlomin have favoured those by Wilf Douglas, C.G. von Brandenstein and Rose Whitehurst, but are grateful for the guidance and support of all Noongar Language material, published or otherwise.

Previous books in UWAP's Wirlomin series have consisted of two blocks of text – one in English, one in Noongar – on each page of print. Feedback suggests this is not ideal. Some thought the Noongar text was too dense. Others, that the English text – intended merely as a guide from which to improvise – was bland and inconsistent. There are indeed challenges bringing an oral tradition to print. With this book we've tried for a narrative voice infused with Aboriginal English, and emphasised Noongar phrases important to ourselves and a wider, regional vernacular.

Thanks to all who attended workshops to develop this story, *Ngalak Yongka Miyak Koorliny*. We begin the story by welcoming our reader and calling on ancestors. The reader is thus placed among various names known to members of our community, from ancestral to newly born, and with numerous nameless others on one of our recurring trips to Yongka Miyak. Glenda Williams and Boydan Coyne deserve particular thanks. Obviously, this book would not exist without their artistic talent, but it also comes from their generous conviviality and commitment. Glenda shared her mother's Noongar language and skilful tongue; said she could tell magpie stories with the bird's own warble. Any rare deviation we make from conventional Noongar spelling is likely an attempt to honour both Glenda and her mother.

Boydan Coyne is a versatile contributor to Wirlomin; he is here as an illustrator, but he is also singer, seed collector and tree-planter at Wilyun Pools, the Wirlomin property near Cape Riche where old Bobby first took up with the expedition and showed Hassell the good grassy land near Yongka Miyak.

Wilyun Pools is where this particular book and its companion,

Wirrawoorliny, began. The property was at one time called 'Black Gins', supposedly for its vast field of ancient grass trees, and is itself only a tiny portion of that stripped for market under the direction years ago to clear a 'million acres a year'. We will never again see such a crowding landscape of grass trees. Acres of plantation timber remain at Wilyun Pools. In collaboration with *Gondwana Link* and others, Wirlomin people collect seeds from remnant vegetation to sow on bare land and among the stumps of blue gum harvests. We scrounge for a share of carbon credits. Graeme Miniter, co-author of this publication and a Wirlomin leader, currently manages Wilyun Pools as a place for cultural and ecological renewal. Despite everything, there remain patches of remnant vegetation and permanent pools in the riverbed. So too with our cultural heritage; we return, consolidate and enhance. And – as with our version of this very old story – we share.

It was from Wilyun Pools that we set off on our most recent trip, *Ngalak Yongka Miyak Koorliny*.

GLOSSARY

Noongar was primarily an oral language before settlers arrived and there are many ways of spelling Noongar words. This book is written using the Marribank spelling style and preferences the south coast dialect.

Ali	all
baalang	our
baalap	they
bardlanginy	travelling
ben	light
bilawin	glittering/shining
bilya	river
biri-k	fingernail-in
boodja	Country/land/ground
boordawan	in the future
boya	rock
demangka	ancestors
demangka-maanga	ancestors
Demi	grandfather
kaalak	home
kaarda	goanna
Kayang	respected old woman
kedelak	night
kenyak	finish
kep	water
koombar	big
koora	before/long ago
koorliny	going/moving
koora koorliny	returning
maya	sound
min-min	moving lights
miyak	moon
miyakelanginy	moon shining
moort	family
ngalak	we
nganang	my
nidja	this/here
nyingarn	echidna
nyininy	sitting/being
toorl	mist
wabiny	playing
wariny	hanging
wirn	spirit
worl-ak	sky-of
wort koorl	away go
yey	now
yira	up
yongka	kangaroo
yoorn	bobtail
yoort-ak	ashes-of
yoowarl koorl	come this way